"This generation of Christians inhabit [a] only biblical revelation about reality but [...]. The Questions for Restless Minds series poses many of the toughest questions faced by young Christians to some of the world's foremost Christian thinkers and leaders. Along the way, this series seeks to help the Christian next generation to learn how to think biblically when they face questions in years to come that perhaps no one yet sees coming."

—**Russell Moore,**
public theologian, *Christianity Today*

"If you're hungry to go deeper in your faith, wrestle with hard questions, and are dissatisfied with the shallow content on your social media newsfeed, you'll really appreciate this series of thoughtful deep dives on critically important topics like faith, the Bible, friendship, sexuality, philosophy, and more. As you engage with some world-class Christian scholars, you'll be encouraged, equipped, challenged, and above all invited to love God more with your heart, soul, mind, and strength."

—**Andy Kim,**
multiethnic resource director, InterVarsity Christian Fellowship

Who Is Jesus of Nazareth?

Questions for Restless Minds

Questions for Restless Minds

How Should Christians Think about Sex? ✦ Christopher Ash

What Does Nature Teach Us about God? ✦ Kirsten Birkett

Who Is Jesus of Nazareth? ✦ Craig L. Blomberg

How Do We Talk with Skeptics? ✦ Sam Chan

What Is the Bible? ✦ Graham A. Cole

What Is a Christian Worldview? ✦ Graham A. Cole

How Do We Know God Exists? ✦ William Lane Craig

What Does It Mean to Be a Thoughtful Christian? ✦ David S. Dockery

Why Does Friendship Matter? ✦ Chris L. Firestone and Alex H. Pierce

Who Chose the Books of the New Testament? ✦ Charles E. Hill

How Do We Live in a Digital World? ✦ C. Ben Mitchell

What Is Islam? ✦ Chawkat Moucarry

Are All Religions True? ✦ Harold A. Netland

How Do Humans Flourish? ✦ Danielle Sallade

How Should We Think about Gender and Identity? ✦ Robert S. Smith

How Can We Help Victims of Trauma and Abuse? ✦ Susan L. and Stephen N. Williams

How Should We Think about Homosexuality? ✦ Mark A. Yarhouse

QUESTIONS FOR RESTLESS MINDS

Who Is Jesus of Nazareth?

Craig L. Blomberg

D. A. Carson,
Series Editor

LEXHAM PRESS

Who Is Jesus of Nazareth?
Questions for Restless Minds, edited by D. A. Carson

Copyright 2021 Christ on Campus Initiative

Lexham Press, 1313 Commercial St., Bellingham, WA 98225
LexhamPress.com

Print ISBN 9781683595298
Digital ISBN 9781683595304
Library of Congress Control Number 2021937697

Lexham Editorial: Todd Hains, Abigail Stocker, Abigail Salinger, Mandi Newell
Cover Design: Brittany Schrock
Interior Design and Typesetting: Abigail Stocker, ProjectLuz.com

The Christ on Campus Initiative exists to inspire students on college and university campuses to think wisely, act with conviction, and become more Christlike by providing relevant and excellent evangelical resources on contemporary issues.

Visit christoncampuscci.org.

Contents

Series Preface ✦ xi

1. Introduction ✦ 1
2. Historic Christian Evidence for Jesus ✦ 9
3. Syncretistic Evidence ✦ 45
4. Remaining Issues ✦ 57
5. Why the Historical Jesus Matters ✦ 69

Acknowledgments ✦ 73
Study Guide Questions ✦ 75
For Further Reading ✦ 77
Notes ✦ 81

Series Preface

D. A. CARSON, SERIES EDITOR

T HE ORIGIN OF this series of books lies with a group of faculty from Trinity Evangelical Divinity School (TEDS), under the leadership of Scott Manetsch. We wanted to address topics faced by today's undergraduates, especially those from Christian homes and churches.

If you are one such student, you already know what we have in mind. You know that most churches, however encouraging they may be, are not equipped to prepare you for what you will face when you enroll at university.

It's not as if you've never known any winsome atheists before going to college; it's not as if you've never thought about Islam, or the credibility of the New Testament documents, or the nature of friendship, or gender identity, or how the claims of Jesus sound too exclusive and rather narrow, or the nature of evil. But up until now you've probably thought about such things within the shielding cocoon of a community of faith.

Now you are at college, and the communities in which you are embedded often find Christian perspectives to be at best oddly quaint and old-fashioned, if not repulsive. To use the current jargon, it's easy to become socialized into a new community, a new world.

How shall you respond? You could, of course, withdraw a little: just buckle down and study computer science or Roman history (or whatever your subject is) and refuse to engage with others. Or you could throw over your Christian heritage as something that belongs to your immature years and buy into the cultural package that surrounds you. Or—and this is what we hope you will do—you could become better informed.

But how shall you go about this? On any disputed topic, you do not have the time, and probably not the interest, to bury yourself in a couple of dozen volumes written by experts for experts. And if you did, that would be on *one* topic—and there are scores of topics that will grab the attention of the inquisitive student. On the other hand, brief pamphlets with predictable answers couched in safe slogans will prove to be neither attractive nor convincing.

So we have adopted a middle course. We have written short books pitched at undergraduates who want arguments that are accessible and stimulating, but invariably courteous. The material is comprehensive enough that it has become an important resource for pastors and other campus leaders who devote their energies to work with students. Each book ends with a brief annotated bibliography and study questions, intended for readers who want to probe a little further.

Lexham Press is making this series available as attractive print books and in digital formats (ebook and Logos resource). We hope and pray you will find them helpful and convincing.

INTRODUCTION

JESUS OF NAZARETH has been the most influential person to walk this earth in human history. Today more than 2.5 billion people worldwide claim to be his followers, more than the number of adherents to any other religion or worldview.[1] Christianity is responsible for a disproportionately large number of the humanitarian advances in the history of civilization—in education, medicine, law, the fine arts, human rights, and even the natural sciences (based on the belief that God designed the universe in an orderly fashion and left clues for people to learn about it).[2] But just who was this individual, and how can we glean reliable information about him? One work on popular images of Jesus in America alone identifies eight quite different portraits: "enlightened sage," "sweet savior," "manly redeemer," "superstar," "Mormon elder brother," "black Moses," "rabbi," and "Oriental Christ."[3] Because these depictions contradict each other at various points, they cannot all be equally accurate. Historians must return to the ancient evidence for Jesus and assess its merits. This evidence falls into three main categories: non-Christian, historic Christian, and syncretistic (a hybrid of Christian and non-Christian perspectives). An inordinate number of websites and blogs make the wholly unjustified claim that Jesus never existed. Biblical scholars and historians who have investigated this issue in detail are virtually unanimous today in rejecting this view, regardless of their theological or ideological perspectives. A dozen or more references to Jesus appear in non-Christian Jewish, Greek, and Roman sources in the earliest centuries of the Common Era (i.e., approximately from the birth of Jesus onward, as Christianity and Judaism began to overlap chronologically). These references appear in such diverse sources as Josephus (a first-century Jewish historian), several different portions of the Talmud (an encyclopedic collection of rabbinic traditions finally, codified in the fourth through sixth centuries), the Greek writers Lucian of Samosata and Mara bar Serapion, and Roman historians Thallus, Tacitus, Pliny, and Suetonius. Tacitus, for example, in the early second century, writes about Nero's persecution of Christians and then explains, "The founder of this name, Christ, had been executed in the reign of Tiberius by the procurator Pontius Pilate."[4] The Talmud repeatedly acknowledges that Jesus worked miracles but refers to him as one who "practiced magic and led Israel astray."[5] Josephus, in the late first century, calls Jesus "a wise man," "a worker of amazing deeds," "a teacher," and "one accused by the leading men among us [who] condemned him to the cross."[6]

It is, of course, historically prejudicial to exclude automatically all Christian evidence, as if no one who became a follower of Jesus could ever report accurately about his life and teachings, or to assume that all non-Christian evidence is necessarily more "objective." But even using only such non-Christian sources, there is ample evidence to confirm the main contours of the early Christian claims: Jesus was a Jew who lived in Israel during the first third of the first century; was conceived out of wedlock; intersected with the life and ministry of John the Baptist; attracted great crowds, especially because of his wondrous deeds; had a group of particularly close followers called disciples (five of whom are named); ran afoul of the Jewish religious authorities because of his controversial teachings, sometimes deemed heretical or blasphemous; was crucified during the time of Pontius Pilate's governorship in Judea (26–36 CE); and yet was believed by many of his followers to have been the Messiah, the anticipated liberator of Israel. This belief did not disappear, despite Jesus' death, because a number of his supporters claimed to have seen him resurrected from the dead. His followers, therefore, continued consistently to grow in numbers, gathering together regularly for worship and instruction and even singing hymns to him as if he were a god (or God).[7]

Contemporary reactions to this composite picture sometimes complain that this seems like a rather sparse amount of information. On the other hand, until the last few centuries, historical and biographical research in general almost exclusively focused on the exploits of kings and queens (or their cultural equivalents), military conquests and defeats, people in official institutional positions of power in a given society; and the wealthy more generally, not least because it was primarily these people who could read or afford to own written documents. Jesus qualified for attention under none of these headings. Moreover, no non-Christians in the first several centuries of the Common Era had any reason to imagine that his influence would grow and spread the way it did in the millennium and half ahead. So it is arguable that it is actually rather impressive that as much has been preserved outside of Christian circles as has been. And of course, most ancient testimony to any person or event has been lost over the centuries, so many other references to Jesus might have existed that we simply no longer know about. The sources that do remain are almost all Greek and Roman documents that weren't writing about events in Israel in the first place.

2

HISTORIC
CHRISTIAN
EVIDENCE
FOR JESUS

B Y FAR THE most important historical information about Jesus of Nazareth appears in the four Gospels of the New Testament. Yet, chronologically, these are not the earliest Christian documents still in existence. Even most conservative scholars acknowledge that the Gospels were not written before the 60s, about thirty years after Jesus was crucified (in either 30 or 33 CE). The majority of the undisputed letters of Paul, however, were all written, at the latest, by the 50s. These include Romans, 1–2 Corinthians, Galatians, and 1 Thessalonians. Thus, when they report on the deeds and sayings of Jesus, they cannot simply be following one or more of the written Gospels for their information. Rather, they must reflect the oral tradition that was preserving those details before the written accounts appeared. The letter of James contains about three dozen probable allusions to the teaching of Jesus, especially from his Sermon on the Mount, and it may well date to as early as the mid-40s.[8] But because this point is more disputed, I will limit our focus here to the epistles of Paul just mentioned before turning to the Gospels themselves.

THE APOSTLE PAUL

Readers of Paul's letters sometimes wonder why he does not refer back to the teachings and deeds of Jesus even more than he does. Several factors no doubt account for this silence. First, he is writing to Christian churches who have already heard considerable details about their Lord. Second, he is dealing primarily with specific issues reflecting the current situations of those congregations. Third, the genre of epistle was not designed primarily to retell the story of the life of Christ. The letters of John, written most likely by the same author as the Gospel of John, barely refer back to specific sayings and events from Jesus' life at all, even though the author had himself written about them in detail. Finally, Christians quickly recognized that the most important features of Jesus' life were his crucifixion and resurrection, and Paul has a lot to say about these in his letters.[9]

Still, it is easy to underestimate the number of quotations and, particularly, allusions to the Jesus tradition in the epistles of Paul, precisely because ancient writers felt free to represent the gist of another person's teaching in their own words. Indeed, in some circles, good rhetoric demanded it. Paul clearly knows the basic outline of Jesus' life.[10]

What Paul appears to know about Jesus is that he was born as a human (Rom 9:5) to a woman and under the law, that is, as a Jew (Gal 4:4), that he was descended from David's line (Rom 1:3; 15:12) though he was not like Adam (Rom 5:15), that he had brothers, including one named James (1 Cor 9:5; Gal 1:19), that he had a meal on the night he was betrayed

(1 Cor 1:23–25), that he was crucified and died on a cross (Phil 2:8; 1 Cor 1:23; 8:11; 15:3; Rom 4:25; 5:6, 8; 1 Thess 2:15; 4:14, etc.), was buried (1 Cor 15:4), and was raised three days later (1 Cor 15:4; Rom 4:25; 8:34; 1 Thess 4:14, etc.), and that afterwards he was seen by Peter, the disciples and others (1 Cor 15:5–7).[11]

More significantly, he knows very specific teachings of Jesus on a wide range of topics. First Corinthians 11:23–25 quotes Jesus' words over the bread and the cup at the Last Supper in considerable detail and in language very close to what Luke later wrote in Luke 22:19–20. Earlier in the same letter, Paul appeals to Jesus' principle that those who preach the gospel should receive their living from the gospel (1 Cor 9:14; compare Luke 10:7; Matt 10:10). He knows that Jesus opposed divorce (1 Cor 7:10; compare Mark 10:2–12) but supported the paying of taxes (Rom 13:7; compare Mark 12:17). He taught about not repaying evil for evil, but rather loving one's enemies and praying for one's persecutors (Rom 12:14, 17–19; compare Luke 6:27–28, 36; Matt 5:38), and about not judging but tolerating one another on morally neutral matters (Rom 14:13; compare Matt 7:1; Luke 6:37). Paul understands that Jesus declared all foods clean (Rom 14:14; compare Mark 7:18–19), that he warned of God's imminent judgment on the leadership of the nation of Israel (1 Thess 2:15–16; compare Matt 23:32–36), and that he predicted numerous specific events in association with his return at the end of the age (1 Thess 4:15–17; 5:2–6; see Christ's discourse on the Mount of Olives in Matt 24–25). These are simply the clearest references in Paul's letters to Jesus' teaching. A much longer list of probable allusions can be compiled.[12] As a result, it just will not do to argue that Paul knew little or nothing about the historical Jesus or that he so distorted his picture of Jesus as to become, for all intents and purposes, the true founder of Christianity.

But we may press the point further. In Paul's most detailed discussion of Jesus' resurrection, he writes,

> Now, brothers and sisters, I want to remind you of the gospel I preached to you, which you received and on which you have taken your stand. ... For what I received I passed on to you as of first importance [or "at the first"]: that Christ died for our sins according to the Scriptures, that he was buried, that he was raised on the third day according to the Scriptures, and that he appeared to Cephas [that is, Peter], and then to the Twelve. After that, he appeared to more than five hundred of the brothers and sisters. (1 Cor 15:1, 3–6)

The language of "receiving" and "passing on" here is technical terminology denoting carefully memorized oral tradition. As central Christian doctrine, Saul of Tarsus (whom we know better as Paul) would have been taught these basic gospel facts not long after his conversion, which took place roughly three years after Jesus' death. Already in that very short period of time, the belief that Jesus was bodily raised from death was entrenched as the heart of the fundamental teaching new converts had to learn. It cannot be chalked up to the slow, evolutionary development of myth or legend decades after the original facts of Jesus' life had been left behind.[13]

THE NEW TESTAMENT GOSPELS

Despite corroborating evidence outside the New Testament Gospels, the bulk of the evidence for Jesus comes from the three Synoptic Gospels (so-called because they are more alike than different and can be set next to each other in parallel columns for easy comparisons among them) and the Gospel of John (which has more differences than similarities to any one of the Synoptics).

THE SYNOPTICS: MATTHEW, MARK, AND LUKE

The various "quests of the historical Jesus" that have proven so influential in the last two centuries of New Testament scholarship have focused primarily on the three Synoptic Gospels.[14] The upshot of all this research is that a significant cross section of current scholarship believes that at least the broad contours and most central items common to Matthew, Mark, and Luke are likely to be historically reliable. Those central themes include such features as the following: Jesus was a Jewish teacher who was raised as a carpenter, but who began a public ministry when he was around the age of thirty. He submitted himself to John's baptism; announced both the

15

present and future dimensions of God's kingdom (or reign) on earth; gave love-based, ethical injunctions to his listeners; taught a considerable amount in parables; challenged conventional interpretations of the Jewish law on numerous fronts but never broke (or taught others to break) the written law; and wrought amazing signs and wonders to demonstrate the arrival of the kingdom. He implicitly and explicitly claimed to be the Messiah or liberator of the Jewish people, but only if they became his followers. And he counterculturally believed that he had to suffer and die for the sins of the world, be raised from the dead, and ascend to his heavenly throne next to Yahweh, only to return to earth at some unspecified point in the future to usher in judgment day. He called all people to repent of their sins and form the nucleus of the new, true, freed people of God, led by his twelve apostles.[15] A number of factors converge to make the assumption probable that a portrait relatively close to this one can be viewed as historically accurate.

Authorship and Date

Many conservative scholars present plausible arguments for accepting the early church's unanimous attributions of the Synoptic Gospels. Mark is a relatively minor character on the pages of the New Testament, probably best known for deserting Paul and Barnabas on their first missionary journey for a reason we are never told (Acts 13:13; 15:37–38). He would not have been a likely person after which to name a Gospel if he did not actually write it, with many other more prominent and respected first-generation Christians available for such an ascription. The same is true of Luke, who was Paul's beloved doctor, but who appears by name only three times in the New Testament, in each case tucked away in the greetings at the end of an epistle (Col 4:14; 2 Tim 4:11; Phlm 24). Matthew, on the other hand, was one of the twelve apostles—Jesus' closest followers during his lifetime—but, as a converted tax collector (Matt 9:9–13), his background could easily have made him the least respected of the Twelve!

Many liberal New Testament scholars nevertheless doubt that Matthew, Mark, and Luke wrote the Gospels bearing their names. But they almost all agree that they were written well within the first century by orthodox Christians in the orbit of apostolic Christianity. Typically suggested dates place Mark in the late 60s or early 70s and Matthew and Luke in the 80s, although occasionally Luke is pushed into the early second century. Conservatives who accept the church fathers' testimony concerning the composition of these Gospels date all three to the early or mid-60s. On either of these main set of dates, however, we are speaking of documents compiled about fifty years or less after the events they narrate. In our age of instant information access, this can seem like a long time. But in the ancient Mediterranean world, it was surprisingly short.

The oldest existing complete biographies of Alexander the Great, for example, are those of Plutarch and Arrian, hailing from the late first and early second centuries CE Alexander died, however, in 323 BCE! Yet classical historians regularly believe they can derive extensive, reliable information from these works to reconstruct in some detail the exploits of Alexander, not least because of the earlier sources these biographers acknowledge utilizing (just like Luke does). This remains true despite various problems in harmonizing certain differences between these two sources and despite certain ideological grids through which each author filtered his information.[16] The words penned over half a century ago by A. N. Sherwin-White, the British historian of ancient Greece and Rome, remain as applicable today as then: "So, it is astonishing that while Graeco-Roman historians have been growing in confidence, the twentieth-century study of the Gospel narratives, starting from no less promising material, has taken so gloomy a turn ... that [for some] the historical Christ is unknowable and the history of his mission cannot be written."[17] This gloom should be replaced by a much more optimistic spirit, as in fact the historical Christ and his mission have been uncovered, little by little, through the solid, painstaking New Testament research that typically doesn't get the attention that the radical fringes do.[18]

Literary Genre

A second issue is that of the Gospels' genre. Did the Synoptic writers intend to produce works that would be viewed as serious histories and biographies by the conventions of their day? The evidence strongly suggests that they did. The clearest indication of what any of the three thought he was doing appears in Luke 1:1–4:

> Many have undertaken to draw up an account of the things that have been fulfilled among us, just as they were handed down to us by those who from the first were eyewitnesses and servants of the word. With this in mind, since I myself have carefully investigated everything from the beginning, I too decided to write an orderly account for you, most excellent Theophilus, so that you may know the certainty of the things you have been taught.

A careful reading of this prologue demonstrates that (1) Luke was aware of previously written sources that documented aspects of the life of Christ; (2) he interviewed eyewitnesses of Jesus' ministry, along with gleaning additional information from others through the oral tradition; and (3) he made his own selection and arrangement of the material in order best to persuade his patron, Theophilus, of the validity of the Christian faith. These are precisely the kinds of details that we find, at times even in very similar language, in the lengthier prologues to volumes of that era which are generally viewed as among the most reliable works of history produced back then—most notably, in the histories of the Jewish author Josephus and of the Greek writers Herodotus, Thucydides, Polybius, and Lucian.[19] Even closer analogies appear in Greco-Roman "technical prose" or "scientific literature," including treatises on such topics as medicine, philosophy, mathematics, engineering, and rhetoric.[20]

All this proves a far cry from the fictitious genres of literature to which modern skeptics often wish to assign the Gospels. Of course, a historical intent by no means guarantees success in accomplishing one's objectives. Indeed, three questions call out for an answer at this point in our investigation. (1) How carefully would the Gospel writers have wanted to preserve historical detail? (2) What ability did they have to do so? (3) How successful were they in their endeavors? With respect to the first question, it is often argued that the compilers of the Gospels would not have had a strong interest in meticulous preservation of accurate detail. Sometimes this conclusion is based on the conviction that words of the risen Lord spoken through early Christian prophets would have been intermingled with the sayings of the earthly Jesus. At other times, it is alleged that a movement that thought that the world might end at any moment would have had no reason to chronicle the life of Jesus with great care. On still other occasions, critics complain that an ideological (in this case, theological) ax to grind necessarily skews one's ability to report objective facts. Let us look at each of these objections in turn.

Authorial Intent

It is true that in first-century Greco-Roman culture, would-be prophets sometimes felt no need to distinguish between the words of a great hero during his life and his later oracles to his followers, speaking (so it was believed) from beyond the grave. But in Jewish tradition, great care was exercised to preserve the correct name of a rabbi to whom a famous teaching was attributed; and, if that information had been lost, attributions were left anonymous. In the New Testament, the only three explicit instances of an early Christian prophet's words (Acts 11:28; 21:10–11; Rev 2:1–3:22) are all clearly distinguished, and distinguishable, from the words of the earthly Jesus. What is more, Paul insisted that all alleged manifestations of the gift of prophecy had to be evaluated by the other Christians present (1 Cor 14:29). From Old Testament days on, one of the central criteria for evaluating supposedly divine words was whether they cohered with previous revelation. So even if some of the teachings in the Gospels did in fact come from later Christian prophets rather than the historical Jesus, the overall portrait of his teaching could not have been materially altered.[21]

The argument about many Christians expecting the imminent end of the world at first glance seems more substantial. The Thessalonian epistles show how Paul had to walk a delicate tightrope between affirming that Christ was coming back soon and yet aknowledging there were signs of the end that had yet to occur. But this was not a new problem for Jesus' followers. Jews, from the time of the first writing prophets in the eighth century BCE onward, had to wrestle with the declaration of Yahweh's spokesmen that the day of the Lord was at hand in a rich variety of ways (e.g., Joel 2:1; Obad 15; Hab 2:3), and yet the centuries continued to march by. The most common solution that pre-Christian Judaism adopted for this dilemma was to cite Psalm 90:4: "A thousand years in your sight are like a day that has just gone by, or like a watch in the night." Second Peter 3:8 shows that New Testament Christianity adopted the same strategy, so that the so-called delay in Christ's return was probably neither the all-consuming issue nor the history-erasing crisis that some have alleged. Moreover, the Essene Jews, responsible for most of the Dead Sea Scrolls discovered at Qumran, lived in the belief that they were seeing end-times events unfold before them, and yet they produced a prodigious literature, including enough information to enable us to chronicle a substantial history of their movement. It is unlikely that the first Christians would have behaved any differently.[22]

What then of the charge that an ideological agenda necessarily biased the Gospels' authors and prevented them from writing adequately objective history? There is no question that ideological bias can create severe historical revisionism: witness the one-line entry under Jesus Christ in the old Soviet Encyclopedia that labeled him the mythological founder of Christianity.[23] More recently, the overtly anti-Semitic president of Iran, Mahmoud Ahmadinejad, seriously questioned whether the Holocaust occurred on anything like the scale it really did, despite the existence of warehouse-sized collections of records attesting the truth. Did the followers of Jesus do something comparable, changing him from a simple Jewish prophet into a cosmic Gentile god?[24] It is not likely. After all, sometimes the very ideology one wants to promote requires careful historical attestation.

Holocaust survivors, like many Jewish historians, were passionately concerned that no comparable genocide ever be perpetrated against their people (or any people) again, and for that very reason painstakingly chronicled atrocity after atrocity. First-century Christianity audaciously claimed that God had acted uniquely in the life, death, and resurrection of Jesus of Nazareth to provide atonement for humanity's sins, reconciliation between those who became his followers and Yahweh, the God of Israel, and the possibility of eternal life in a recreated and perfected universe in the future. If Christianity's opponents had been able to show that the central elements of the New Testament data did not closely resemble the true facts about Jesus, this fledgling religion would have crumbled at once. Or as Paul puts it quite simply, "If Christ has not been raised, your faith is futile; you are still in your sins" (1 Cor 15:17). In sum, the Gospel writers had every reason to want to preserve accurate history.

Compositional Procedures

Were they able to do so? Even if a thirty-year oral tradition was remarkably short by ancient standards, it still leaves plenty of time for distortion to creep in, perhaps even unwittingly and undetected. Can we seriously believe that documents written no earlier than the early 60s accurately recounted the deeds and teachings of Jesus in the late 20s or early 30s? As it turns out, we can. Ancient Jews honed the art of memorization to an amazing extent. Some rabbis had the entire Hebrew Scriptures committed to memory. A few had quite a bit of the oral Torah (the oral law) under command as well.[25] A scribe who had recently completed a new copy of the Torah would often have the most gifted or venerated local rabbi proofread his manuscript by checking it against that rabbi's memory!

Nor were these feats limited to Jews in the ancient Mediterranean world. Greek schoolboys (and, unfortunately, with rare exceptions it was only schoolboys in both Jewish and Gentile contexts) sometimes committed either the Iliad or the Odyssey—Homer's epic poems that functioned much like Scripture in Greek circles—to memory, with each containing between 130,000 and 160,000 words. How was such memorization possible? First, the ancient Mediterranean world was made up of oral cultures not dependent on all the print media that dominate our modern world. Second, the main educational technique employed in schools was rote memorization. Jews even had a tradition that schoolchildren needed to memorize a passage of the Torah before they discussed it, lest they perhaps misrepresent it. Third, in Jewish circles, "Bible" was the only subject students studied during the fairly compulsory elementary education that spanned ages five to twelve or thirteen, and that took place wherever there were large enough Jewish communities to have a synagogue. Fourth, memorization thus would begin at an early age when it is the easiest period of life to master large amounts of content. Fifth, texts were often sung or chanted; the tunes helped students remember the words as they do with contemporary music, too. Finally, a variety of other mnemonic devices dotted the texts that were studied so intensely. Especially crucial in the Jewish Scriptures were numerous forms of parallelism between lines, couplets, and even larger units of thought. In this kind of milieu, accurately remembering and transmitting the amount of material found in one Gospel would have been comparatively easy.[26]

At the same time, mere memorization cannot be the only factor that lies behind the transmission of the Gospel tradition. If it were, we would not have four different Gospels; or, if we did, they would not vary in the precise ways that they do. It has long been recognized that the Synoptic Gospels almost certainly reflect some kind of literary relationship among themselves. That is to say, one or more of these three documents utilized one or more of the others or other common sources. Only in this fashion can we account for the extensive, verbatim parallelism between corresponding accounts of the same event, interspersed with utterly unparalleled or only partially paralleled material. A few conservative scholars have argued for complete independence, leaving only divine inspiration to account for the current combination of similarities and differences, but this flies in the face of Luke's own testimony in Luke 1:1–4 and the standard Jewish and Greco-Roman practices of writing histories and biographies.

Most Gospels scholars therefore believe that, at least in the finished forms in which we now have them, (1) Mark came first, (2) Matthew and Luke each independently relied on Mark wherever they wanted to, and (3) Matthew and Luke each utilized additional sources, both written and oral. One of these may well have been a common source, primarily of sayings of Jesus, to which both Matthew and Luke had access in view of the approximately 250 verses in these two Gospels common to each other but not found in Mark. This hypothetical source has come to be called Q (from the German word *Quelle*, for "source").[27]

Another factor comes into play here, too, which recent research has been particularly scrutinizing. Prior to a text becoming "canonical"—uniquely sacred and authoritative in written form—revered traditions in ancient Mediterranean cultures were transmitted orally with certain flexibility within fixed limitations. Even into the late twentieth century, preliterate or semiliterate communities or people groups in as diverse locations as Africa, the Balkan states, Lebanon, and Palestine appointed certified "tradents"— oral storytellers (or singers) who were responsible for regularly rehearsing or performing the sacred traditions of that group of people. Yet, far from repeating every last word identically with each retelling of the epic, anywhere from 10–40 percent of the actual words could vary from one occasion to the next. This allowed for varying selections of episodes and portions of episodes to include abbreviation, explanation, application, and paraphrase, in part for the storyteller to demonstrate some creative artistry and in part to keep the audience's interest fresh. At the same time, 60–90 percent of the information remained unvarying, including all elements deemed necessary for the lessons of the stories to remain intact. Tradents who left out or garbled any of these elements were to be interrupted and corrected by those in the audience who recognized the mistakes.[28]

Now turn back to the Synoptic Gospels. Choose all of the passages unambiguously appearing in at least two of these three books. That is to say, limit yourself to accounts that the various Gospel writers assign to the same time or place that cannot be dismissed as Jesus simply doing two somewhat similar things twice or teaching the same basic message in different contexts. Count the words that are identical in the Greek in the parallel accounts. Rarely will you find less than 10 percent or more than 40 percent of the words differing! What has been called "informal controlled oral tradition" has almost certainly been at work in the production of the Synoptics and not just verbatim memorization and literary dependence on previously written sources.[29] This kind of tradition does not produce verbatim reproduction of every minor word but is true to the details that make a story or a teaching what its author intended it to be.

Nor dare we underestimate the power of the community in a culture that did not at all value individualism the way we do. Bart Ehrman likens the oral transmission of the Gospel tradition to the children's game of telephone, in which a long and complex message is whispered to one child who then has the responsibility of whispering what he or she thinks the message was to the next child, and so on.[30] After this "tradition" has been passed on to a number of participants, even over the span of a few minutes, the final child who then speaks out loud the last version of the message usually draws hilarious laughter because of how garbled the message has become. But Ehrman could hardly have chosen a more irrelevant analogy. The Gospel traditions were not whispered but publicly proclaimed, not to children but to adults, in the presence of knowledgeable tradents or with apostolic checks and balances (see, for example, how Peter and John function in Acts 8:14–17). Indeed, a burgeoning field of research in the social sciences today is scrutinizing how "social memories" of various subcultures are formed through repetition and interpretation in community, creating certain fixed forms of oral tradition that might well not otherwise be established.[31] Even apart from this trend, Kenneth Bailey's research tellingly demonstrated that playing "telephone" with groups of his adult

Middle-Eastern students did not yield garbled messages but extraordinarily well preserved ones![32] This is exactly what we should expect of the Gospels too, given the culture in which they emerged.

Apparent Contradictions

So the first Christian generation had plenty of reasons to want to preserve accurate information about Jesus. They certainly had the ability to do so as well. But did they succeed in accomplishing their objectives? The main obstacle to affirming that they did succeed involves the apparent contradictions between parallel accounts of episodes in Christ's life. Space does not permit us to look at anything like a comprehensive list of these seeming problems.[33] But the vast majority of them fall into predictable categories.

The largest group simply reflects the natural variations in storytelling and writing that characterize most partially independent accounts of the same event, without calling into question the historicity of the event itself. Many involve inclusion (or omission) of those details most relevant (or irrelevant) to a given Gospel writer's purposes, particularly his theological emphases. Only rarely do these create dramatic differences between two parallels, but even then we can understand how both perspectives may remain true. For example, were the disciples still misunderstanding Jesus due to hard hearts after he walked to them on the water on the Sea of Galilee (Mark 6:52), or did they worship him and call him the Son of God (Matt 14:33)? It takes only a little imagination to put ourselves in their position and see how acts of worship and titular acclamation, each without much understanding or truly empathetic hearts, would be a natural reaction. And once we learn that the disciples' failures and misunderstandings are a recurrent theme in Mark, while Matthew tends to portray their moments of greater faith and worship more often, we can see why each writer has chosen to narrate things the way he has.

Some of the most dramatic apparent contradictions simply involve different conventions for reporting events in the ancient world. Does the centurion himself come to ask for Jesus to heal his servant (Matt 8:5–9), or does he send his friends (Luke 7:1–8)? Presumably the latter, because it was perfectly natural to speak of someone saying or doing something even if it actually occurred through duly appointed agents. The same is still true in certain modern contexts, as, for example, when a press secretary reads to the media what a speech writer has composed, yet news reports maintain that "the President today said …" Does Jairus come to ask Jesus to heal his daughter while she is still alive, only to find out later that she has just died (Mark 5:22–23, 35), or does he come only after her death (Matt 9:18)? Because Matthew regularly abbreviates Mark's longer stories, he has probably also done so here, so that Mark gives the fullest, most accurate detail. But even if Matthew does not satisfy modern, scientific standards of precision, it is unfair to impose those standards on a first-century world that had not yet invented them. None of the differences affect the point of the story, which is the miraculous resurrection of the girl.

For some reason, one of the more popular recurring charges of contradiction between Gospel parallels involves the identity of those individuals seen by the women who went to Jesus' tomb early on that Sunday morning we now celebrate on Easter. Mark 16:5 has them seeing a young man dressed in a white robe, Matthew 28:2–3 refers to an angel with clothing white as snow, while Luke 24:4 speaks of two men in dazzling apparel. Since angels are regularly depicted in the Bible as men, often in white or shining clothing, there is no reason that Mark or Luke needed to mention explicitly that angels were present. As for the number of them, if there were two it would hardly be inaccurate to say that the women saw a young man who spoke to them, especially if one was the consistent spokesperson for the two. Only if Mark or Matthew had said that the women saw one person all by himself would there be an actual contradiction.[34]

Ehrman describes his own personal pilgrimage when, after writing a paper in graduate school harmonizing Mark's reference to Abiathar as the high priest in the account of David eating the sacred showbread (Mark 2:26) with the clear statement in the Old Testament that says it was Ahimelech (1 Sam 21:1–6), his professor asked him why he couldn't just admit that Mark made a mistake. This, Ehrman claims, then opened the floodgates for him to recognize the Bible as nothing but a human book with errors all over the place.[35]

Ironically, this "all or nothing" approach is exactly what some ultraconservatives have (illogically) insisted on as well. But no historian of any other ancient document operates this way. A document that has proved generally reliable is not suddenly discounted because of just one demonstrable mistake. At the same time, it is not at all clear that Mark did make a mistake. The expression he uses in the Greek is a highly unusual one if he meant to indicate time, since the preposition *epi* that he places before Abiathar's name normally means over, on top of, on, near, toward, or some other word denoting location.[36] But in Mark 12:26, when an identical construction appears in the context of Jesus' recounting the story of Moses and the burning bush, most translations render the Greek "in the passage" or "in the account" of the bush. Probably, in 2:26 Mark likewise intended Jesus to be understood as referring to the passage about Abiathar. Of course, this raises the follow-up objection that Abiathar doesn't appear in 1 Samuel until chapter 22. But ancient Judaism divided Scripture into "passages" according to how much was read each week in the synagogues in order to get through all of the Law annually and all of the rest of the Old Testament once every three years. This required several chapters to be grouped together as a "passage" in most cases. Moreover, we know that each passage was given a brief title, often based on the name of a key character in it, and that overall Abiathar was a better known figure than Ahimelech. So it would not be unusual if a several-chapter stretch of 1 Samuel had been labeled "Abiathar." We cannot prove this, but it is plausible enough that we need not resort to assuming that Mark just made a mistake.[37]

We could continue giving numerous examples akin to these that we have treated briefly. Some of the proposed solutions are no doubt more persuasive than others. Some seeming discrepancies have more than one possible solution, and different interpreters may opt for differing proposals as the most plausible. Occasionally, one runs across a problem where none of the proposed solutions seems free from difficulties. A lot depends at this juncture on how much benefit of the doubt one is willing to give the Gospel writers. Completely apart from any presuppositions about whether a certain text is inspired or not, historians regularly seek for credible harmonizations, along lines very similar to those we have illustrated, when they encounter seemingly contradictory testimony in ancient works that have established themselves elsewhere as reasonably competent and in a position to be "in the know."[38] It is not as if any of the problem passages are new—Christians have been aware of them for two millennia. Both Augustine in the fifth century and Calvin in the sixteenth wrote detailed commentaries on harmonies of the Gospels and regularly addressed the texts that skeptics today find problematic. More conservative contemporary commentaries, along with scholarly monographs and articles, contain plausible solutions for every "error" that skeptics can list. People whose faith is shaken as easily as Ehrman suggests his was over the supposed discovery of a solitary error must be looking for reasons to abandon their faith, rather than engaging in dispassionate, historical investigation.

In sum, we may affirm that the Synoptic Gospel writers would have wanted to preserve accurate history according to the standards of their day, that they had every likelihood of being able to do so, and that the overall pattern of widespread agreement on the essential contours of Jesus' life and ministry, coupled with enough variation of detail to demonstrate at least some independent sources and tradents on which each drew, makes it very probable that they did in fact compose trustworthy historical and biographical documents. Certainly no insoluble contradictions appear.

THE GOSPEL OF JOHN

But what about the Fourth Gospel? Here the differences with the Synoptics appear to outweigh the similarities. Noticeably more passages in John than not find no parallel in Matthew, Mark, or Luke. John contains no parables, no exorcisms, and almost no teaching about the kingdom, and he fails to mention that Jesus was baptized by John or that he instituted the Lord's Supper during the last meal of his earthly life with his disciples. On the other hand, John contains two chapters about Jesus' ministry before the major period of popularity with the Galilean crowds that dominates the Synoptics (John 2–4). During that period of popularity he focuses primarily on Jesus' trips to Jerusalem at festival time, which are entirely absent from the Synoptics, and the claims he made for himself and the conflicts he precipitated with various Jewish leaders there, along with his most spectacular miracle of all—the resurrection of Lazarus (John 5–11). Throughout his ministry, John's Jesus makes the most explicit references of anywhere in the canonical Gospels to his own exalted nature, implying his deity. For all these and related reasons, many scholars, including those open to a fair amount of history in the Synoptics, are often more skeptical of the historical trustworthiness of John. Is this skepticism justified?

General Considerations

For much of church history, Christians simply assumed that John, as the last and latest of the four New Testament Gospels, saw no need to repeat what was covered well in the Synoptics and intended largely to supplement their narratives. However, in the early twentieth century—the heyday of biblical source criticism—scholars observed that even when John and the Synoptics did include parallel accounts of the same event, very few exact words were ever repeated, much different from the results of a comparison of parallels among the Synoptics. So the pendulum swung to the opposite conviction: John was so different from the Synoptics because he wrote independently of them, whereas Matthew, Mark, and Luke were related to each other at least partly via some form of literary dependence. For a little more than the last twenty years, a mediating perspective has been increasingly promoted that may well do the most justice to the most data: By the end of the first century, most

Christians around the empire would have been familiar with the main accounts that the Synoptics retold, whether they had ever heard an actual copy of Matthew, Mark, or Luke read aloud to them in church or not. So, while John does seem to be literarily independent of the Synoptics, the older argument about him not needing to repeat a lot of what they treated well may be reinstated too.[39]

John's unique setting also accounts for much of his distinctive contents. Good early church tradition ascribes this Gospel to the aged apostle, brother of James and son of Zebedee, writing from Ephesus to the Christian churches in and around that community who were experiencing the twin challenges of an increasingly hostile Judaism that excommunicated synagogue members who confessed Jesus as Messiah and of an incipient Gnosticism that had no problem affirming Jesus' deity but denied his true humanity. Thus we should not be surprised to see John stressing how Jesus was indeed the fulfillment of major Jewish festivals and rituals (as in John 5–10), despite the conflict that it caused with the religious leadership of his people. The loftier claims about his deity (especially 1:1) may well have been John's way of establishing common ground with those overly influenced by the Gnostics, with a needed corrective emphasis on how "the Word became flesh and made his dwelling among us" (1:14).[40]

A particularly intriguing phenomenon that demonstrates how much more both John and the Synoptists actually knew and how complementary, rather than contradictory, their Gospels are has sometimes been called their "interlocking."

This phenomenon involves instances in which John refers to something so cryptically as to raise all kinds of questions that he nowhere else answers but that the Synoptics do, or vice versa. For example, John 3:24 refers in passing to John the Baptist's imprisonment, but only the Synoptists ever narrate that event (Mark 6:14–29 and parallels). John knows Jesus was tried before the high priest Caiaphas (John 18:24, 28), but only the Synoptics describe this trial's proceedings or its outcome (Mark 14:53–65 and parallels). Conversely, the Synoptists assert that witnesses twisted Jesus' words to accuse him of claiming that he would destroy the temple and rebuild it in three days (Mark 14:57–58). But nothing elsewhere in their narratives prepares the reader for this charge. John 2:19, on the other hand, includes Jesus' allegation that if the Jewish leaders destroyed "this temple," he would rebuild it in three days; but it goes on to explain that he was speaking of the temple of his body, that is, an allusion to his death and resurrection. This, however, is a saying that could easily be twisted into what the Synoptics claim the false witnesses declared. Or again, why did the Jewish leaders enlist the help of the Roman governor, Pilate (Mark 15:1–3 and parallels), when their law was clear enough in prescribing the death penalty—by stoning—for blasphemers? Only John gives us the answer: under Roman occupation the Jews were forbidden from carrying out this portion of their law (John 18:31). Many more examples of such interlocking, in both directions, can be adduced.[41]

Specific Passages

We may also proceed sequentially through the Fourth Gospel, noting strong historical reasons for accepting at least a solid core of most of the main episodes as authentic, including those unique to this Gospel. Distinct to John 1 is the desctription of the period in which Jesus' ministry overlaps with John the Baptist's before Jesus clearly outshines his predecessor. The early church is unlikely to have invented a time when John needed to "become less" so that Christ could "become greater" (John 3:30), as concerned as they were to exalt Jesus over everyone. John 2 begins with the remarkable miracle of turning water into wine, yet it coheres perfectly with the little parable in the Synoptics of new wine (Jesus' kingdom teaching) needing new wineskins (new religious forms), regularly viewed as authentic. John 3 highlights Jesus' conversation with Nicodemus, a rare Jewish name that appears repeatedly in rabbinic literature with reference to a number of individuals over several generations in the wealthy, powerful, Pharisaic ben Gurion family. The story of Jesus' surprising concern for the Samaritan woman in John 4 coheres closely with his compassion for outcasts throughout the Synoptics. The distinctive synagogue homily in John 6 on Jesus as the bread of life matches perfectly with a standard rabbinic exegetical form known as a proem midrash. Jesus' claims at the Festival of Tabernacles to be living water and the light of the world (in John 7–9) fit exactly two central rituals from that feast—a water-drawing ceremony and daily temple services with a giant candelabrum installed just for this occasion. One could continue in similar fashion throughout the Gospel, identifying key reasons for the probable authenticity of a critical core of each main segment.[42]

What then of apparent contradictions between John and the Synoptics? Many of them may be dealt with via a similar cross section of the methods applied to the seeming discrepancies among the Synoptics. Quite a few have to do with Mark's choice to include only one visit of the adult Jesus to Jerusalem, at the Passover during which he was crucified—a choice that Matthew and Luke then followed. It is inherently probable that his ministry lasted longer than the few months it would have taken to do everything the Synoptics record, and, as a Jew who kept the written laws of Moses, Jesus would have surely attended the various annual festivals in Jerusalem prescribed in the Torah. Indeed, John appears more consistently chronological in the sequence of his accounts than do the Synoptists, who often group material together by theme or form, especially during Jesus' great Galilean ministry. Because Jesus' resurrection of Lazarus took place in Judea just before Jesus' final journey to Jerusalem, once the Synoptists had decided on their outlines, this miracle simply did not fit into them. Parables may have been omitted from John because they were a uniquely Jewish form less relevant in Ephesus, to which John's Gospel was written according to early church tradition. Exorcisms may have been left out because they

39

were often viewed more as manipulative religious "magic" in the Greco-Roman world. The concept of the kingdom is largely replaced by the theme of eternal life, but this is a legitimate substitution because already in Matthew 19:16, 23–24, Jesus uses them interchangeably.

It is often alleged that John and the Synoptics contradict each other over the day of the Last Supper. The Synoptics clearly describe it as a Passover meal (e.g., Mark 14:12, 14, 16), whereas it is often alleged that John places it the day before the beginning of the Passover festival (especially in light of John 13:1, 29; 18:28; 19:14, 31). But when John 13:1 explains "it was just before the Passover Feast" (NIV 1984) and then a verse later refers simply to the evening meal in progress, it is at least as natural to assume that the Passover has now arrived as that this is a different, earlier meal. When Judas leaves the meal and the other disciples think he is going to buy "what was needed for the feast" (John 13:29, NIV 1984), he could easily be thought to be securing provisions for the rest of the week-long festivities, especially since some also thought he was going "to give something to the poor," precisely a tradition central to the opening evening of Passover. That the Jewish leaders on Friday morning do not want to defile themselves because of the upcoming Passover meal (John 18:28) suggests that the midday meal is in view rather than that evening's dinner, since a new day started at sundown in Jewish reckoning and removed the defilement of the previous day. John 19:14 is often translated "It was the day of Preparation of the

Passover" but it could equally be rendered, "It was the day of Preparation during Passover week"—that is, the Friday of Passover week, because Friday was the day of preparation for the Jewish Sabbath or Saturday. Verse 31 actually supports this interpretation since it explicitly declares that the next day was to be a Sabbath. So again, a more careful reading of the text undermines the charge of contradictions.[43]

What then of John's high Christology—his exalted view of Jesus which frequently equates him with God? We must always remember that statements from the lips of Jesus that sound so exalted to us with twenty-twenty hindsight, such as "I am the light of the world," "the true vine," "the sheep gate," "the good shepherd," "the way and the truth and the life," or "the resurrection and the life," were all metaphors that did not initially communicate without ambiguity. Even John's appeal to the divine "I AM" of Exodus 3:14 (John 8:58) no doubt puzzled many. After all, the Twelve could remark as late in Jesus' ministry as the last night of his life that only then was he finally "speaking clearly and without figures of speech" (John 16:29). Even then, Jesus' reply, anticipating their reaction to his death, suggests that they still do not fully understand (16:31–32). Conversely, only the Synoptics narrate the virginal conception, which clearly represents high Christology. And they too have Jesus using the language of "I am," sometimes masked in translation by the English "I am he" or "It is I." But in passages like Mark 6:50, in the context of his walking on the water, or Mark 14:62

as he replies to the Sanhedrin concerning his messiahship, it is hard not to believe that a stronger self-revelation of his divinity is not being at least hinted at.[44]

Topography and Archaeology

Intriguingly, while John is the most overtly theological of the canonical Gospels, it also supplies the greatest amount of geographical information about the locations where events occur. Precisely because such references do not reflect John's main purposes in writing (see John 20:31 for those), they are all the more significant when they consistently turn out to be historically accurate. Most sites can still be visited today, and archaeological discoveries disproportionately illuminate John's Gospel compared to the Synoptics: the pool of Bethesda with its five porticoes near the Sheep Gate in Jerusalem (John 5:2), the pool of Siloam in Jerusalem (9:7), Jacob's well at Sychar (4:5–6), the paving stones of Gabbatha (19:13), inscriptional evidence for Pontius Pilate (18:29), evidence of Roman use of nails through the ankles for crucified victims (compare Luke 24:39 with John 20:25), and the like.[45]

Literary Genre

There is no question that on a spectrum from bare, uninterpreted historical chronicle to total fiction, John stands a little further removed from the former extreme than do the Synoptics.[46] John uses his own linguistic style in recounting Jesus' words, so that at times it is almost impossible to know where Jesus stops speaking and John starts narrating (see, classically, 3:13–21). In keeping with historiographical conventions of the day, he is often more overtly theological than the Synoptists. But in terms of literary genre, his work remains closer to Matthew, Mark, and Luke in form than to any other known writing of the ancient Mediterranean world. And a strong case has been made that this form most closely mirrored relatively trustworthy biographies.[47] A passage-by-passage comparison of John with the Synoptics points out conceptual parallels at almost every juncture, even if they do not reflect literary dependence and even if they are often narrated in a more dramatic fashion. The very emphasis of John's Gospel on providing trustworthy testimony to the truthfulness of the Christian message (21:24–25) makes its historical reliability that much more important and probable.

3

SYNCRETISTIC EVIDENCE

BLOCKBUSTER WORKS OF fiction like *The Da Vinci Code* have misled many readers because of erroneous claims that in it "all descriptions of ancient documents are accurate."[48] As a result, countless people around the world now believe that various non-canonical documents present an alternate story of Christian origins that has a greater historical likelihood of being reliable. In fact, nothing could be further from the truth. Particularly intriguing have been the Gnostic gospels, so we will deal with them first and then turn to other post-New Testament apocryphal documents.

THE GNOSTIC GOSPELS

Just after World War II, a cache of codices was unearthed in Egypt at a site known as Nag Hammadi. Ranging from the second to the sixth centuries in origin, a sizeable majority of these books reflected elaborate Gnostic influence. Gnosticism was a collection of loosely related religious movements that combined significant elements of Greek philosophy and ritual with Christian characters and themes to create a hybrid, syncretistic mythology. At the heart of these various movements lay the conviction that matter is inherently evil and thus that only a person's spirit can be redeemed. Redemption, it was often believed, came through Jesus, but not through his atoning death and bodily resurrection. Rather salvation came by knowledge—esoteric knowledge, to be more precise. Humans who recognized the spark of divinity deeply embedded in themselves and who fanned it into flame could then become initiates into a Gnostic sect, living as already somewhat free from the shackles of the body and the material world while looking forward to escaping this world and their bodies altogether upon death. Most Gnostics, therefore, were ascetics, trying to deny themselves normal bodily appetites, although a few swung the pendulum to the opposite extreme and became hedonists, indulging the body since they would soon be rid of it anyway. Most Gnosticism was anti-Semitic, rejecting the God of Israel as evil and the laws of the Israelites as perverse. It was also elitist, believing that no one in whom the gods had not already planted the spark of divinity could ever be saved.[49]

THE GOSPEL OF THOMAS

If there is any Gnostic gospel likely to preserve historical information about Jesus outside of texts that simply repeat information already found in the canonical Gospels, it is the so-called Coptic Gospel of Thomas. Though fourth century in origin in its Nag Hammadi form, second-century Greek fragments of it had already been discovered in nineteenth-century archaeological excavations at Oxyrhynchus. Thomas is not a connected narrative biography but a collection of 114 mostly independent sayings attributed to Jesus. A little over a third find some reasonably discernible parallel in the canonical texts, roughly another third seem fairly clearly Gnostic in meaning, and the remaining sayings are those that often fascinate scholars the most. Might there be authentic teachings of Jesus in this mix, not preserved elsewhere? There certainly could be, but how would one ever discern which ones they are? After all, presumably all of Thomas's sayings could be interpreted in a Gnostic fashion, so it would be hard to develop fool-proof criteria for sifting the authentic from the inauthentic.

Those who have made educated guesses as to which passages might go back to Jesus often include sayings 82 ("He who is near me is near the fire, and he who is far from me is far from the kingdom") and 77b ("Split a piece of wood, and I am there. Lift up the stone, and you will find me there") or the little parables of the woman carrying a jar of meal (saying 97) and the man who stuck his sword into the wall (saying 98).[50] They read, respectively: "Jesus said, 'The kingdom of the father is like a certain woman who was carrying a jar full of meal. While she was walking on a road, still some distance from home, the handle of the jar broke and the meal emptied out behind her on the road. She did not realize it; she had noticed no accident. When she reached her house, she set the jar down and found it empty.'" And "Jesus said, 'The kingdom of the father is like a certain man who wanted to kill a powerful man. In his own house he drew his sword and stuck it into the wall in order to find out whether his hand could carry through. Then he slew the powerful man.'"[51]

Accepting a few such sayings, however, hardly revolutionizes our portrait of Jesus. To argue that Gnosticism (or any other form of heterodoxy) actually predates orthodox, apostolic Christianity requires dating Thomas (or other texts) into the mid-first century without any actual documentary evidence or external testimony supporting such a date. In fact, Nicholas Perrin has maintained that the structure of Thomas, based on catchwords linking each saying to the next, appears most clearly in its Syriac form, which is dependent on *Harmony of the Gospels* written by a Syrian named Tatian in about 180 CE. So Thomas may well not date to any earlier a date than this.[52] Even if it does, the fact that it contains parallels to every one of the four canonical Gospels, and all of the putative sources and layers of editing that scholars typically identify behind them, strongly suggests that Thomas was not composed until the second century, by which time all four canonical texts were complete and had begun to circulate widely. Scholars like Elaine Pagels, Karen King, and others often support a Thomasine or Gnostic form of Christianity over traditional forms because they believe that such religion proves more affirming of women.[53]

Some texts do appear to promote a form of egalitarianism based on the belief that we will one day all become androgynous as we were, so it is asserted, in the beginning of human history. But this supports only the feminism of a generation ago, which blurred the distinctions between male and female in the name of equal opportunity, rather than the currently dominant form that insists on equality within difference. Moreover, one has to read the Gnostic literature very selectively to get even a partial egalitarianism. Consider, for example, the final saying in Thomas:

> Simon Peter said to him, "Let Mary leave us, for women are not worthy of life." Jesus said, "I myself shall lead her in order to make her male, so that she too may become a living spirit resembling you males. For every woman who will make herself male will enter the kingdom of heaven" (Thomas 114).[54]

The vast majority of women, in any age, do not consider this an attractive option!

OTHER GNOSTIC GOSPELS

Very few other Nag Hammadi documents even overlap in contents with the canonical texts at all. Those that are called gospels are usually collections of lengthy, esoteric monologues attributed to Jesus after the resurrection in secret conversation with one or more of the disciples about the nature of heavenly beings and entities, far removed from the down-to-earth, practical ethics of Jesus of Nazareth. In keeping with Gnosticism's rejection of the full humanity of Jesus, little interest in his earthly life appears. Instead, the documents that are falsely ascribed to such writers as Philip, Mary, James, and others devote almost all their attention to speculation about Jesus' heavenly origins and relationships, the nature of humanity in its fallenness and in redemption, parallel realities between earth and heaven, and the like.[55]

A partial exception is the more recently discovered Gospel of Judas. It actually does appear in narrative form, though in its fragmentary condition it covers only select events from the last week of Jesus' life; and, as we already knew from the writings of Irenaeus (the bishop of Lyons, France, at the end of the second century), it makes Judas the hero, rather than the villain, in betraying Christ. Despite his ignominious end on earth, he will be exalted in heaven, since someone had to turn Jesus over to the authorities so that he could atone for the sins of the world. Of course, the logic is flawed; there are countless ways Jesus could have been put to death. And it represents a tiny minority viewpoint, even among ancient Gnostics. Despite the surprisingly sensationalized and occasionally inaccurate presentation of the contents of this gospel by the National Geographic Society in 2006,[56] even very liberal and non-Christian biblical scholars quickly concede that there is no chance that this reflects the original version of events.[57]

OTHER APOCRYPHAL GOSPELS

From the mid-second century of Christianity onward, other "gospels" appeared as well. Many of these have survived, some only in partial form, while others are known only because various early Christian writers, or occasionally their opponents, make mention of them. Most of these appear to respond to the natural curiosity of readers of the New Testament about the "gaps" in the gospel record. What was Jesus like as a child? The Infancy Gospel of Thomas, not to be confused with the Coptic Gospel of Thomas, portrays him as a boy wonder, fashioning birds out of clay and breathing into them the breath of life so that they might fly away or, more ominously, withering up a playmate who refused to stop taunting him. The Protevangelium of James describes Mary's "immaculate conception"—that is, the belief that her parents were completely free from lust when they conceived her, enabling her to become sinless. They also describe a truly virgin birth—even after Jesus came out of Mary's womb, the midwives confirmed that her hymen remained unbroken! At the other end of Jesus' life, the Gospel of Nicodemus contains a narrative of Christ's descent into hell, while the Gospel of Peter embellishes the resurrection account, with Christ emerging from the tomb accompanied by two angels, one on either side of him, whose heads reached up to the heavens, while Christ's went through the heavens! Almost no true historians believe these documents came from the people to whom they are ascribed or that they reflect genuine, historical events not found in the New Testament.[58]

Still other documents are sometimes falsely put forward as being of ancient pedigree, when in fact they were written in the Middle Ages or even more recently. The Gospel of Barnabas is a medieval Muslim composition that teaches explicitly Islamic doctrine and even contradicts the Qur'an in places (e.g., in denying Christ's messiahship).[59] More orthodox Christian texts purport to disclose never before seen documents written by Jewish and Roman leaders who participated in the proceedings against Jesus (most notably in a nineteenth-century composition called the Archko Volume, which is sheer modern fiction). The Book of Mormon addresses a particularly troubling theological issue of the early nineteenth century—the fate of the native Americans before their evangelization by European settlers—by claiming to be the long hidden account of the exploits of Jews and their descendants who migrated to the Americas centuries before Christ, and containing the story of the supposed appearance of Jesus to people on this continent not long after his death and resurrection in Israel. Per Beskow discusses the true origins of many of these and similar stories.[60] At the very least, we may insist that those who are inclined to be suspicious of portions of the New Testament Gospels have no historical reason for placing any confidence in these extracanonical sources.

A quick exercise comparing the New Testament Gospels and Gnostic/apocryphal gospels, using a number of standard historical criteria, proves remarkably telling. The canonical texts are all first century in origin, no more than two generations removed from the eyewitnesses of Jesus' life; no other gospel can be demonstrated to be earlier than the mid-second century, at least two generations later. Most are one to five centuries later! The literary genres of the canonical Gospels closely resemble ancient historiography and biography, while not one of the Gnostic texts contains more than short bits of narrative in it, and most do not have any. The apocryphal texts are typically written in connected prose, but none purports to cover more than a tiny slice of Jesus' life or ministry. Except for some elements in the Gospel of Thomas, there are no problems of harmonization because the kinds of things that Jesus says or does in the apocrypha are so unlike the canonical Jesus that one must choose which one to accept (if either)—they cannot both be right! The canonical Gospels leave no doubt that Jesus of Nazareth was a human being. The issue his followers struggled with was how to account for his teachings and miracles, and they were increasingly compelled to use the language of deity. The Gnostic and at least some of the apocryphal gospels have absolutely no question about the deity of a spirit-being called Christ, but whether that spirit ever was (or could have been) fully human is very much open to question. There is no archaeological corroboration for any distinctive parts of the Gnostic or apocryphal gospels because, for the most part, their contents do not include events or sayings tied to any particular place. There is no testimony from non-Christian sources to support them, not least because they were not well enough known to command others' attention.[61] All of these observations prove crucial as we turn to two key remaining objections that often prove to be stumbling blocks for people in accepting the New Testament message.

4

REMAINING
ISSUES

I OFTEN ENCOUNTER QUESTIONS along the following lines: How do we even know that we have what the authors of the canonical Gospels first wrote? Haven't the texts been copied so many times, with so many errors having crept in, that what Matthew, Mark, Luke, and John first wrote might have been quite different? Add to that all the different translations, especially in English, from the ancient Greek, and surely even more corruption has intruded, hasn't it? Even if this first cluster of questions can be dealt with, isn't it the case that the Gospels included in the New Testament canon are simply the product of ecclesiastical politics? Only because orthodoxy ultimately won out over Gnosticism do we have the Bible we have instead of a very different one. So how can anyone claim that these are uniquely inspired and authoritative sources for belief and behavior? The first of these clusters of questions deals with issues of text and translation; the second, with the formation of the canon. We shall consider each, briefly, in turn.

TEXT AND TRANSLATION

About 5,300 handwritten Greek manuscripts of part or all of the pre-Gutenberg New Testament remain in existence.[62] These range from a scrap of a few verses to entire copies of the New Testament. We have an unbroken sequence of ever growing textual resources (in both numbers and amount of text represented) from the early second century until the invention of the printing press in the fifteenth century. Overall, the texts were copied with remarkable care; the vast majority of changes that were introduced involved variant spellings, the accidental omission or repetition of a single letter, the substitution of one word for a synonym, and the like. Textual critics of almost all theological stripes agree that we can reconstruct somewhere upwards of 97 percent of the New Testament text beyond a shadow of reasonable doubt. And it is certainly the case that no Christian belief or doctrine depends solely on a textually disputed passage. All these factors set the New Testament books off from every other known work from the ancient world in terms of our ability to have confidence that we know what the original authors wrote.[63] Bart Ehrman's *Misquoting Jesus* (see note 35) chooses to focus entirely on the tiny handful of more interesting and significant textual variants and could mislead the careless reader into thinking such changes occurred more often than they did, but even Ehrman acknowledges that we have enough textual evidence that we can sift the most probable original readings from the later changes. As for translations, the differences among all the major English versions have to do merely with linguistic philosophy—how literal or paraphrastic a rendering is (or, more technically, how formally or dynamically equivalent). A comparison of any dozen of the major Bible translations makes it clear how amazingly minor the overall differences are; again, all the fundamentals of the faith clearly appear in all of these versions.[64]

THE FORMATION OF THE NEW TESTAMENT CANON

In the mid-second century, Christian writers began to compile lists of books they believed were canonical—that is, uniquely accurate and authoritative and worth putting on a par with the Hebrew Scriptures (what Christians would come to call the Old Testament). At first, this occurred largely in response to unorthodox teachings like those the various Gnostic sects promoted. But what is intriguing is that we have no record of the Gnostics themselves ever proposing any of their distinctive documents for inclusion in any canon, theirs or anyone else's. Instead, they tried to reinterpret New Testament writings in a fashion that would support their distinctives for the very reason that they recognized the unique authority attached to those documents. As the decades went by, the number of books for a New Testament on which there was agreement grew, until in 367 CE, in his Easter encyclical, bishop Athanasius of Alexandria listed the twenty-seven books that have ever since comprised the canon. Ecumenical councils in both Carthage and Hippo, in North Africa, at the end of the fourth century ratified this common consensus. As far as we know, the four Gospels, Acts, and the letters of Paul were never seriously in doubt. The only significant debates surrounded the letters of Hebrews, James, 2 Peter, 2–3 John,

Jude, and the book of Revelation. And the only books that were ever serious candidates for inclusion in the New Testament but were omitted were also epistles from the second-century collection of largely orthodox Christian writings known as the Apostolic Fathers. Even then, there was considerably more enthusiasm for the most weakly supported of the letters that did make it in than for any of those that were left out. In no meaningful sense did these writers, church leaders, or councils suppress Gnostic or apocryphal material, since there is no evidence of any canon that ever included them, nor that anyone put them forward for canonization, nor that they were known widely enough to have been serious candidates for inclusion had someone put them forward. Indeed, they would have failed all three of the major criteria used by the early church in selecting which books they were, at times very literally, willing to die for—the criteria of apostolicity (that a book was written by an apostle or a close associate of an apostle), coherence (not contradicting previously accepted Scripture), and catholicity (widespread acceptance as particularly relevant and normative within all major segments of the early Christian community).[65]

MIRACLES AND THE RESURRECTION

For some readers, potentially sympathetic to much of what we have already affirmed, the key sticking point remains the question of the supernatural. However strong the rest of the evidence may be, can we take seriously the historical claims of any documents as full of accounts of the miraculous as the canonical Gospels, and especially when so much hinges on the veracity of the most spectacular alleged miracle of all, namely, Jesus' resurrection? The largest part of an answer to this question lies outside the scope of this short book because it involves the much broader question of worldview. Is there reason to believe in a God who created the universe in the first place? If there is, then miracles arguably become possible and perhaps even likely. Has science truly demonstrated that the universe is a closed continuum of cause and effect? If so, then we must exclude the miraculous, at least as normally conceived.

What can be noted here as we near the conclusion of this book is that other ancient documents sometimes contain miracle narratives that don't preclude historians, whatever their views of the supernatural, from deriving sober historical detail from many other portions of those works. A striking example involves the four existing accounts of Julius Caesar's crossing of the Rubicon River, committing himself to the civil war that would lead to his becoming emperor and turning the republic into an empire. Often alluded to as one of the most historical (and historic) of events found in ancient Mediterranean sources, it is nevertheless accompanied in some accounts by miraculous apparitions (along with problems of harmonization and dating remarkably parallel to those among the New Testament Gospels). Yet classicists who reject the supernatural still confidently recover substantial historical information from all these accounts.[66]

Biblical scholars who are open to the supernatural are often accused of adopting a double standard: they will accept various miraculous stories in the Bible but not in other works of ancient history. This would indeed be a double standard if their only rationale for such judgments were the sources in which the various accounts appeared. But often the corroborating evidence simply remains stronger for the biblical accounts.[67] On the other hand, there are a small number of claims of the miraculous at numerous junctures throughout history that do pass stringent criteria of authenticity, and there is no reason that Christian scholars should not accept them as well. God, in the Bible, often works through those who are not his people; human manufacture and diabolical influence are also possible sources for apparent miracle-working power.[68] It is telling, moreover, to observe how often the closest parallels to canonical Gospel miracles appear in later Jewish or Greco-Roman sources, so that if any tradition influenced any other one, it would be Christianity being "copycatted" later. Demonstrably pre-Christian traditions do not present close parallels to the New Testament Gospels' miracles at all.[69]

In today's world, there is actually an extraordinary amount of evidence for events parallel to every major category of New Testament miracle, but especially to healings and exorcisms, on every continent on the globe. Craig

Keener has amassed reports of thousands of such miracles and has published the documentation for several hundred of the most securely attested and verified ones in his prodigious two-volume work on miracles. He has also catalogued a handful of reasonably undeniable resurrections.[70] When one sees a consistent pattern, that these have occurred after public, concerted, Christian prayer, it is hard to deny a correlation. The claim that such miracles should then be predictable, however, does not follow. Jesus makes it clear that God does not work signs on demand to satisfy the skeptic (compare Matt 16:1–4). If he did, we would have religion by formula and the power of God by manipulation. And the events would cease to be considered miraculous.[71] This is what sociologists of religion call "magic" rather than "miracle."[72] God always leaves enough evidence to make belief rational but also leaves enough reason to doubt so that faith can never be said to be coerced.

As for the topic of the resurrection in particular, again an entirely separate book is needed to do it justice. But we may at least note here that several undisputed historical facts are very difficult to explain apart from Jesus' genuine, bodily return to life, including (1) how a small band of defeated followers of Jesus were transformed, almost overnight, into bold witnesses, risking death by proclaiming his bodily resurrection before many of the same people who fifty days earlier had participated in his crucifixion; (2) what motivated a group of devoted Jews to change what they believed to be the eternally immutable Sabbath (or day of rest and worship) from Saturday to Sunday; (3) why did they claim in all versions of their testimony that women, whose witness was usually inadmissible in ancient law courts, were the first and primary witnesses to the empty tomb; (4) what led them to declare Jesus to be both Lord and liberator despite his death by crucifixion, a kind of death already interpreted, in light of Deuteronomy 21:23, to represent God's curse; and (5) how the Jewish expectation of all people being raised from the dead together at the end of time (Dan 12:2) allowed them to declare Jesus to have been raised in advance of judgment day and separate from the general resurrection. It takes more faith to believe the various alternative accounts of the rise of the resurrection traditions than to accept them as retold in the New Testament.[73]

5

WHY THE
HISTORICAL JESUS
MATTERS

I F THE CANONICAL Gospels remain our only source for more than just a barebones outline of the life and work of Jesus of Nazareth as a truly human figure and if there are good reasons on sheer historical grounds, apart from any religious faith, to accept the main contours of their portraits of Jesus as historically trustworthy, then the "step of faith" involved in acknowledging Jesus as Lord and Savior and committing one's life in service and allegiance to him become the most reasonable responses a person can make to his ministry. History cannot corroborate everything in these Gospels, but it can provide enough support so that a spirit of trust rather than of suspicion remains natural in those areas where more difficult questions arise. The testimony of millions upon millions of Christians' lives, transformed for the better—who often get far less press than the comparatively small number of believers responsible for the more shameful deeds done throughout history in Jesus' name, provides powerful experiential confirmation of the value of choosing to align ourselves with him. To receive forgiveness of sins, to be put into a right relationship with God, to understand one's vocation in this life as counting for all eternity, and to look forward to unending happiness in the life to come in the very presence of God in Christ and in all the company of his people throughout time, all form powerful motivations for entrusting oneself to Jesus despite the ignominy, suffering, and even martyrdom that such commitment can at times lead to in this world. The alternative, which is unending separation from God and all things good precisely because God refuses to coerce belief or to give people that which they reject (including himself and his salvation), certainly makes any unpleasant aspects of this life pale in comparison.

Acknowledgments

T HE SERIES Questions for Restless Minds is produced by the Christ on Campus Initiative, under the stewardship of the editorial board of D. A. Carson (senior editor), Douglas Sweeney, Graham Cole, Dana Harris, Thomas McCall, Geoffrey Fulkerson, and Scott Manetsch. The editorial board recognizes with gratitude the many outstanding evangelical authors who have contributed to this series, as well as the sponsorship of Trinity Evangelical Divinity School (Deerfield, Illinois), and the financial support of the MAC Foundation and the Carl F. H. Henry Center for Theological Understanding. The editors also wish to thank Christopher Gow, who created the study questions accompanying each book, and Todd Hains, our editor at Lexham Press. May God alone receive the glory for this endeavor!

Study Guide Questions

1. How would you tell the story of the life of Jesus?

2. What point is Blomberg making in his comparison of the historical record of the life of Alexander the Great and that of the life of Jesus?

3. What does the prologue of Luke tell us about his intention in writing his Gospel?

4. What point does Blomberg make by emphasizing the communal environment in which the stories of the Gospel were passed down? Can you think of a better analogy for the passing on of the textual tradition than "telephone" that includes something like "social memory"?

5. What do you make of the point that Calvin (sixteenth century) and Augustine (fifth century) addressed the same texts that modern skeptics find problematic for harmonizing the Gospel accounts?

6. How would you explain the concept of "interlocking" as it relates to harmonizing John's Gospel with the synoptic accounts?

7. Are there any lingering questions you have about harmonization or canonization? What are some texts that you have found historically difficult in the past? Does this book provide methods of interpretation that can help you understand them?

8. Blomberg makes the case that the Christian faith and witness to Jesus points not only to spiritual truth but also to historical events. How does this message change the way you read your Bible or relate to the person of Jesus?

For Further Reading

Blomberg, Craig L. *The Historical Reliability of John's Gospel: Issues and Commentary*. IVP, 2001.

_____. *The Historical Reliability of the Gospels*. 2nd ed. IVP, 2007.

Bock, Darrell L. *The Missing Gospels: Unearthing the Truth Behind Alternative Christianities*. Nelson, 2006.

An excellent introduction to the beliefs of Gnosticism and other ancient mutations of Christianity deemed heretical, showing just how different and inferior they really are to historic Christianity when considered as entire worldviews.

Bowman, Robert M., Jr. and J. Ed Komoszewski. *Putting Jesus in His Place: The Case for the Deity of Christ*. Kregel, 2007.

Debunks in detail the myth that first-century Christians did not, almost uniformly, believe in the deity of Christ, from the earliest stages of the New

Testament onward. Makes a strong case for believing that Jesus *was* indeed divine.

Boyd, Gregory A. and Paul R. Eddy. *Lord or Legend? Wrestling with the Jesus Dilemma.* Baker, 2007.

An abbreviated and more popular-level form of their larger work, *The Jesus Legend: A Case for the Historical Reliability of the Synoptic Jesus Tradition* (Baker, 2007). Covers all the most important issues succinctly while fully abreast of the whole range of recent scholarship.

Evans, Craig A. *Fabricating Jesus: How Modern Scholars Distort the Gospels.* IVP, 2006.

A careful sifting of all of the sources outside the New Testament alleged by some to enable us to view the historical Jesus in radically different terms than the four canonical Gospels present. In short, the conclusion is that they fail in this endeavor.

Jones, Timothy P. *Misquoting Truth: A Guide to the Fallacies of Bart Ehrman's "Misquoting Jesus."* IVP, 2007.

A point-by-point refutation of the misleading claims of Ehrman's book, *plus* an equally helpful critique of his books on the so-called lost gospels and lost Christianities. Surveys a huge amount of scholarship and presents it in a remarkably readable, bite-size fashion.

Roberts, Mark D. *Can We Trust the Gospels? Investigating the Reliability of Matthew, Mark, Luke, and John*. Crossway, 2007.

In many ways, without obviously intending to do so, a simplified and very popularized form of almost the identical array of issues I treat in my book, *The Historical Reliability of the Gospels*, for those who find even my semipopularization of the issues too daunting.

Notes

1. Mary Fairchild, "How Many Christians Are in the World Today?" *Learn Religions* (April 16, 2020), https://www.learnreligions.com/christianity -statistics-700533.

2. See especially Jonathan Hill, *What Has Christianity Ever Done for Us? How It Shaped the Modern World* (IVP, 2005). Compare David Bentley Hart, *Atheist Delusions: The Christian Revolution and Its Fashionable Enemies* (Sheridan, 2009), 111–215.

3. Stephen Prothero, *American Jesus: How the Son of God Became a National Icon* (Farrar, Straus & Giroux, 2003).

4. Tacitus, Annals 44:3, in Robert E. Van Voorst, *Jesus Outside the New Testament: An Introduction to Ancient Evidence* (Eerdmans, 2000), 45.

5. Babylonian Sanhedrin 43a, Van Voorst, *Jesus Outside the New Testament*, 113.
   11.15, Babylonian Shabbath.

6. Antiquities of the Jews 18.3.3, Van Voorst, *Jesus Outside the New Testament*, 84.

7. The most thorough and evenhanded presentation and assessment of these data appears in Van Voorst, *Jesus Outside the New Testament* (Eerdmans, 2000). Peter Schäfer is particularly helpful, from a Jewish perspective, on the clear references and various additional possible allusions in the rabbinic literature (*Jesus in the Talmud* [Princeton University Press, 2007]). What Josephus originally wrote has been disputed, but a reasonable consensus suggests that the only Christian interpolations were to affirm Jesus' messiahship and resurrection rather than simply note his followers' allegations (see Alice Whealey, *Josephus and Jesus: The Testimonium Flavianum Controversy from Late Antiquity to Modern Times* (Peter Lang, 2003).

8. Peter H. Davids, *The Epistle of James* (Eerdmans, 1982), 22, 47–48. See Alicia J. Batten, "The Jesus Tradition and the Letter of James," *Review and Expositor* 108 (2011): 381–90.

9. See further Craig L. Blomberg, *Making Sense of the New Testament: Three Crucial Questions* (Baker, 2004), 71–103.

10. See especially Gary Knoppers, "The Synoptic Problem: An Old Testament Perspective," *Bulletin for Biblical Research* 19 (2009): 11–34

11. Stanley E. Porter, "Images of Christ in Paul's Letters," in *Images of Christ: Ancient and Modern,*

ed. Stanley E. Porter, Michael A. Hayes and David
Tombs (Sheffield Academic, 1997), 98–99.

12. Craig L. Blomberg, "Quotations, Allusions, and
Echoes of Jesus in Paul," *Studies in the Pauline Epistles: Festschrift for Douglas J. Moo*, ed. Matt Harmon
and Jay Smith (Zondervan, 2014), 129–43.

13. Striking support for these claims appears in the
work of atheist historian Gerd Lüdemann (with
Alf Özen), *What Really Happened to Jesus? A Historical Approach to the Resurrection* (Westminster
John Knox, 1995), 15. See also Carl Stecher ("The
Historical Evidence is Insufficient and Contradictory," in *Resurrection: Faith or Fact?* by Carl Stecher
and Craig Blomberg, with Richard Carrier and
Peter S. Williams [Pitchstone, 2019], 53), who
accepts the premise that followers of Jesus were
reporting their belief in his resurrection within two
years of his death.

14. See Colin Brown, "The Quest for the Historical
Jesus," in *Dictionary of Jesus and the Gospels*, 2nd ed.,
ed. Joel B. Green, Jeannine K. Brown, and Nicholas Perrin (IVP Academic, 2013), 718–56.

15. See especially Martin Hengel and Anna Maria
Schwemer, *Jesus and Judaism* (Baylor University
Press, 2019). See also Robert L. Webb and Darrell
L. Bock, eds., *Key Events in the Life of the Historical
Jesus: A Collaborative Exploration of Context and*

Coherence (Eerdmans, 2010); and Craig S. Keener, *The Historical Jesus of the Gospels* (Eerdmans, 2009).

16. Craig L. Blomberg, "The Legitimacy and Limits of Harmonization," in *Hermeneutics, Authority, and Canon,* ed. D. A. Carson and John D. Woodbridge (Zondervan, 1986), especially 169–73. Compare Soo Kwong Lee, "Source Criticism of Accounts of Alexander's Life with Implications for the Gospels' Historical Reliability," in *Biographies and Jesus: What Does It Mean for the Gospels to Be Biographies?,* ed. Craig S. Keener and Edward T. Wright (Emeth, 2016), 201–16.

17. A. N. Sherwin-White, *Roman Society and Roman Law in the New Testament* (Oxford University Press, 1963), 187. Much more recently, see throughout Craig S. Keener, *Christobiography: Memory, History, and Reliability of the Gospels* (Eerdmans, 2019).

18. See especially James H. Charlesworth and Petr Pokorný, with Brian Rhea, eds., *Jesus Research,* 2 vols. (Eerdmans, 2009–14); and Tom Holmén and Stanley E. Porter, eds., *Handbook for the Study of the Historical Jesus,* 4 vols. (Brill, 2011).

19. A. W. Mosley, "Historical Reporting in the Ancient World," *New Testament Studies* 12 (1965): 10–26; Terrence Callan, "The Preface of Luke-Acts and Historiography," *New Testament Studies* 31 (1985): 576–81. See also Craig S. Keener, "Assumptions in Historical Jesus Research: Using Ancient Biog-

raphies and Disciples' Traditioning as a Control,"
Journal for the Study of the Historical Jesus 9 (2011):
26–58.

20. Loveday C. Alexander, *The Preface to Luke's Gospel:
Literary Convention and Social Context in Luke 1.1–4
and Acts 1.1* (Cambridge University Press, 1993).

21. See further Ben Witherington III, *Jesus the Seer:
The Progress of Prophecy* (Hendrickson, 1999),
293–328.

22. See further Charles L. Holman, *Till Jesus Comes:
Origins of Christian Apocalyptic Expectation* (Hendrickson, 1996).

23. I. Howard Marshall, *I Believe in the Historical Jesus*
(Eerdmans, 1977), 15.

24. As was the thesis of Maurice Casey, *From Jewish
Prophet to Gentile God: The Origins and Development of New Testament Christology* (Westminster
John Knox, 1991).

25. For those who find these claims hard to believe,
the popular twentieth-century Jewish writer
Chaim Potok liked to tell of similar, verified feats
of learning among Orthodox Jewish students in the
yeshivas of New York City.

26. For all these and related practices, see especially
Birger Gerhardsson, *Memory and Manuscript: Oral
Tradition and Written Transmission in Rabbinic
Judaism and Early Christianity* (1961, 1964; repr.,
Eerdmans, 1998); Birger Gerhardsson, *The Reliabil-*

ity of the Gospel Tradition (Hendrickson, 2001). See also Alessandro Vatri, "Ancient Greek Writing for Memory: Textual Features as Mnemonic Facilitators," *Mnemosyne* 68 (2015): 750–73. For the most detail, see Rainer Riesner, *Jesus als Lehrer: Einer Untersuchung zum Ursprung der Evangelien-Überlieferung,* 2nd ed. (J. C. B. Mohr, 1988).

27. An excellent introduction to Gospel source criticism, as this exercise is called, which presents the various hypotheses that have been proposed with the major rationales for each, is Robert H. Stein, *Studying the Synoptic Gospels: Origin and Interpretation,* 2nd ed. (Baker, 2001). This volume also deals nicely with the features of oral tradition and with the final editing of the canonical Gospels. For other important options, along with the majority view, see Stanley E. Porter and Bryan R. Dyer, eds., *The Synoptic Problem: Four Views* (Baker, 2016).

28. Two of the most important researchers and their most important works have been Albert B. Lord, *The Singer of Tales,* 2nd ed. (Harvard University Press, 2000); and Jan Vansina, *Oral Tradition as History* (University of Wisconsin Press, 1985). For application to the Gospels, see especially James D. G. Dunn, *The Oral Gospel Tradition* (Eerdmans, 2013); Rafael Rodriguez, *Structuring Early Christian Memory: Jesus in Tradition, Performance and Text* (T&T Clark, 2010); and T. M. Derico, *Oral*

Tradition and Synoptic Verbal Agreement: Evaluating the Empirical Evidence for Literary Dependence (Pickwick, 2016).

29. Kenneth E. Bailey, "Informal Controlled Oral Tradition and the Synoptic Gospels," *Asia Journal of Theology* 5 (1991): 34–54.; reprinted in *Themelios* 20 (1995): 4–11. Bailey's work was later vigorously critiqued by Theodore J. Weeden, "Kenneth Bailey's Theory of Oral Tradition: A Theory Contested by Its Evidence," *Journal for the Study of the Historical Jesus* 7 (2009): 3–43. But the fallacies of Weeden's critique were highlighted by Craig S. Keener, "Weighing T. J. Weeden's Critique of Kenneth Bailey's Approach to Oral Tradition in the Gospels," *Journal of Greco-Roman Christianity and Judaism* 13 (2017): 41–78.

30. Bart D. Ehrman, *Jesus: Apocalyptic Prophet of the New Millennium* (Oxford University Press, 1999), 51–52.

31. Nicely summarized and supplemented by Richard Bauckham, *Jesus and the Eyewitnesses: The Gospels as Eyewitness Testimony,* 2nd ed. (Eerdmans, 2017), 319–57.

32. Kenneth E. Bailey, "Middle Eastern Oral Tradition and the Synoptic Gospels," *Expository Times* 106 (1995): 563–67.

33. But see Craig L. Blomberg, *The Historical Reliability of the Gospels,* 2nd ed. (IVP, 2007), 152–95; and

Darrell L. Bock and Benjamin I. Simpson, *Jesus according to Scripture: Restoring the Portrait from the Gospels,* 2nd ed. (Baker, 2017).

34. For an excellent analysis of all of the so-called contradictions surrounding the various accounts of Christ's resurrection, see John W. Wenham, *Easter Enigma: Do the Resurrection Stories Contradict One Another?* (Zondervan, 1984).

35. Bart D. Ehrman, *Misquoting Jesus: The Story Behind Who Changed the Bible and Why* (HarperSanFrancisco, 2005), 9.

36. Not until the eighteenth and final cluster of definitions given by Walter Bauer et al., eds., *A Greek-English Lexicon of the New Testament and Other Early Christian Literature,* 3rd ed. (University of Chicago Press, 2000), 367, does a temporal usage ("in the time of") appear.

37. See especially John W. Wenham, "Mark 2.26," *Journal of Theological Studies* 1 (1950): 156.

38. See throughout my "Legitimacy and Limits of Harmonization," 139–74. See also Vern Sheridan Poythress, *Inerrancy and the Gospels: A God-Centered Approach to the Challenges of Harmonization* (Crossway, 2012); and Lydia McGrew, *The Mirror or the Mask? Liberating the Gospels from Literary Devices* (DeWard, 2019).

39. See especially Richard Bauckham, "John for Readers of Mark," in *The Gospels for All Christians:*

Rethinking the Gospel Audiences, ed. Richard Bauckham (Eerdmans, 1998), 147–71. See also Edward W. Klink III, *The Sheep of the Fold: The Audience and Origin of the Gospel of John* (Cambridge University Press, 2007), 157–81; and my modifications of Klink's and Bauckham's approach in Craig L. Blomberg, "The Gospels for Specific Communities and All Christians," in *The Audience of the Gospels: The Origin and Function of the Gospels in Early Christianity*, ed. Edward W. Klink III (T&T Clark, 2010), 111–33.

40. See further Craig L. Blomberg, *The Historical Reliability of John's Gospel: Issues and Commentary* (IVP, 2001), 17–67; compare Jey J. Kanagaraj, *John* (Cascade, 2013), 5–7.

41. See especially Leon Morris, *Studies in the Fourth Gospel* (Eerdmans, 1969), 40–63; D. A. Carson, *The Gospel According to John* (1991), 52–55.

42. See especially my *Historical Reliability of John's Gospel*, 71–81; compare Richard Bauckham, *The Testimony of the Beloved Disciple: Narrative, History, and Theology in the Gospel of John* (Baker, 2007); *John, Jesus, and History, Volume 2: Aspects of Historicity in the Fourth Gospel*, ed. Paul N. Anderson, Felix Just, and Tom Thatcher (SBL, 2009); Stanley E. Porter, *John, His Gospel, and Jesus: In Pursuit of the Johannine Voice* (Eerdmans, 2015).

43. See further Barry D. Smith, "The Chronology of the Last Supper," *Westminster Theological Journal* 53 (1991): 29–45; Cullen I. K. Story, "The Bearing of Old Testament Terminology on the Johannine Chronology of the Final Passover of Jesus," *Novum Testamentum* 31 (1989): 316–24; and Norval Geldenhuys, *The Gospel of Luke* (Eerdmans, 1951), 649–70.

44. In addition to my writings elsewhere, for the kinds of interpretations of texts utilized in this subsection, see especially Craig S. Keener, *The Gospel of John: A Commentary,* 2 vols. (Hendrickson, 2003); and Edward Klink, III, *John* (Zondervan, 2016).

45. For the Gospels overall, see especially James H. Charlesworth, ed., *Jesus and Archaeology* (Eerdmans, 2006). Emphasizing the Gospels' accuracy in light of archaeology is Bargil Pixner, *Paths of the Messiah: Messianic Sites in Galilee and Jerusalem* (Ignatius, 2010). On John's Gospel in particular, compare James H. Charlesworth with Jolyon G. R. Pruszinski, eds., *Jesus Research: The Gospel of John in Historical Inquiry* (T&T Clark, 2019), 97–185.

46. See especially Derek Tovey, *Narrative Art and Act in the Fourth Gospel* (Sheffield Academic, 1997). See Jo-Ann A. Brant, *Dialogue and Drama: Elements of Greek Tragedy in the Fourth Gospel* (Baker, 2004).

47. See especially Richard A. Burridge, *What Are the Gospels? A Comparison with Graeco-Roman Biography*, 25th anniv. ed. (Baylor University Press, 2018). For an appreciative survey of Burridge's influence, see Steve Walton, "What Are the Gospels? Richard Burridge's Impact on Scholarly Understanding of the Genre of the Gospels," *Currents in Biblical Research* 14 (2015): 81–93. For a broader overview of recent opinion, see Judith A. Diehl, "What Is a 'Gospel'? Recent Studies in the Gospel Genre," *Currents in Biblical Research* 9 (2011): 171–99.

48. Dan Brown, *The Da Vinci Code* (Doubleday, 2003), 1. Sometimes apparently historical finds turn out to have been hoaxes, as with the fragments of the so-called Secret Gospel of Mark and the so-called Gospel of Jesus' Wife. Sometimes genuine historical finds are misinterpreted or misidentified, as with the so-called Jesus' Family Tomb.

49. Excellent introductions to Gnosticism from different perspectives include Alastair H. B. Logan, *The Gnostics: Identifying an Early Christian Cult* (T&T Clark, 2006); Riemer Roukema, *Jesus, Gnosis and Dogma* (T&T Clark, 2010); and Nicola Denzey Lewis, *Introduction to "Gnosticism": Ancient Voices, Christian Worlds* (Oxford University Press, 2013).

50. *Gospel of Thomas*, trans. Thomas O. Lambin, Coptic Gnostic Library Project of the Institute for

Antiquity and Christianity, http://www.gnosis.org/naghamm/gthlamb.html

51. Lambin, *Gospel of Thomas.* Excellent, comparatively recent commentaries on the Coptic Gospel of Thomas include Uwe-Karsten Plisch, *The Gospel of Thomas: Original Text with Commentary* (Hendrickson, 2008); Petr Pokornỳ, *A Commentary on the Gospel of Thomas: From Interpretations to the Interpreted* (T&T Clark, 2009); and Simon Gathercole, *The Gospel of Thomas: Introduction and Commentary* (Brill, 2014).

52. Nicholas Perrin, *Thomas, the Other Gospel* (Westminster John Knox, 2007), 73–106. Simon Gathercole (*The Composition of the Gospel of Thomas: Original Language and Influences* [Cambridge University Press, 2012]) has contested this, arguing that Greek is the original language but it still shows persuasively that Thomas is second century and dependent on the canonical Gospels. See also Mark Goodacre, *Thomas and the Gospels: The Case for Thomas's Familiarity with the Synoptics* (Eerdmans, 2012).

53. Elaine Pagels, *Beyond Belief: The Secret Gospel of Thomas* (Vintage Books, 2003); and Karen L. King, ed., *Images of the Feminine in Gnosticism* (Trinity Press International, 1988). See also April D. deConick, *The Gnostic New Age: How a Countercultural*

Spirituality Revolutionized a Religion from Antiquity to Today (Columbia University Press, 2016).

54. Lambin, *Gospel of Thomas.*

55. See especially Majella Franzmann, *Jesus in the Nag Hammadi Writings* (T&T Clark, 1996).

56. Rodolphe Kasser, Marvin Meyer, and Gregor Wurst, eds., *The Gospel of Judas* (National Geographic Society, 2006).

57. Such as Bart D. Ehrman, *The Lost Gospel of Judas Iscariot: A New Look at Betrayer and Betrayed* (Oxford University Press, 2006), 172–73.

58. The standard, critical English translation of an introduction to all the noncanonical gospels (of which we know) is Wilhelm Schneemelcher, ed., *New Testament Apocrypha*, vol. 1, 2nd ed. (Westminster John Knox, 1991). For a very helpful, more accessible introduction to both the Gnostic and non-Gnostic works without the texts themselves, see Markus Bockmuehl, *Ancient Apocryphal Gospels* (Westminster John Knox, 2017). Standing almost alone in defending part of the Gospel of Peter as older and more trustworthy than the canonical texts is John Dominic Crossan, *The Cross That Spoke: The Origins of the Passion Narrative* (Harper & Row, 1988).

59. Oddbjørn Leirvik, "History as a Literary Weapon: The Gospel of Barnabas in Muslim-Christian

Polemics," *Studia Theologica* 54 (2001): 4–26; Jan Joosten, "The Gospel of Barnabas and the Diatessaron," *Harvard Theological Review* 95 (2002): 73–96.

60. Per Beskow, *Strange Tales about Jesus: A Survey of Unfamiliar Gospels* (Fortress, 1983).

61. See Craig L. Blomberg, "Canonical and Apocryphal Gospels: How Historically Reliable Are They?" *From Athens to Jerusalem* 6.3 (2006): 1–7. The one exception is a reference to one of the Infancy Gospel's miracles in the Qur'an, attesting to the heterodoxy of at least some of the Christians with whom Muhammad came into contact.

62. Jacob W. Peterson, "Math Myths: How Many Manuscripts We Have and Why More Isn't Always Better," in *Myths and Mistakes in New Testament Textual Criticism,* ed. Elijah Hixson and Peter J. Gurry (IVP, 2019), 68–69. Many sources list higher numbers, even upwards of 5,800. For the problems with such numbers and the need to risk erring on the side of caution, see the rest of Peterson's chapter (pages 48–69).

63. For sample comparative statistics, see Darrell L. Bock and Daniel B. Wallace, *Dethroning Jesus: Exposing Popular Culture's Quest to Unseat the Biblical Christ* (Nelson, 2007), 31; or J. Ed Komoszewski, M. James Sawyer, and Daniel B. Wallace, *Reinventing Jesus: What The Da Vinci Code and*

Other Novel Speculations Don't Tell You (Kregel, 2006), 71. The most up-to-date figures, with analyses about how they are ascertained, appear throughout *Myths and Mistakes,* ed. Hixson and Gurry. This volume is now by far the most reliable and wide-ranging source for avoiding the kinds of mistakes apologists and other non-specialists, including myself, have too often made.

64. See Craig L. Blomberg, *Can We Still Believe the Bible? An Evangelical Engagement with Contemporary Questions* (Brazos, 2014), 83–118. For the rationales for the kinds of differences that do appear, compare Gordon D. Fee and Mark L. Strauss, *How to Choose a Translation for All Its Worth: A Guide to Understanding and Using Bible Versions* (Zondervan, 2007). An exception to this principle of the value of all versions is the Jehovah's Witnesses' New World Translation, which mistranslates the Greek at those places where the New Testament contradicts their doctrine in order to hide this fact from their readers. Paraphrases, of course, by design take greater liberties with the text. Occasionally, a paraphrase will try to hide this fact by claiming to be a translation, as with the recent *Passion Translation* of the New Testament, Psalms, Proverbs, and Song of Solomon.

65. For full details on this history see especially F. F. Bruce, *The Canon of Scripture* (IVP, 1988). For

the various lists and catalogs of New Testament collections from the early centuries, see appendix D in *The Canon Debate,* ed. Lee M. McDonald and James A. Sanders (Hendrickson, 2002), 591–97. See also Michael Kruger, *Canon Revisited: Establishing the Origins and Authority of the New Testament Books* (Crossway, 2012).

66. Paul Merkley, "The Gospels as Historical Testimony," *Evangelical Quarterly* 58 (1986): 328–36.

67. For application to the Gospels, see especially Graham H. Twelftree, *Jesus the Miracle Worker* (IVP, 1999); René Latourelle, *The Miracles of Jesus and the Theology of Miracles* (Paulist, 1988); and selected chapters in Graham H. Twelftree, ed., *The Nature Miracles of Jesus: Problems, Perspectives, and Prospects* (Cascade, 2017).

68. See further Joseph Houston, *Reported Miracles: A Critique of Hume* (Cambridge University Press, 1994).

69. See further Craig L. Blomberg, *Can We Still Believe in God? Answering Ten Contemporary Challenges to Christianity* (Brazos, 2020), 65–83.

70. Craig S. Keener, *Miracles: The Credibility of the New Testament Accounts,* 2 vols. (Baker, 2011); Craig S. Keener, "'The Dead Are Raised' (Matthew 11:5 // Luke 7:22): Resuscitation Accounts in the Gospels and Eyewitness Testimony," *Bulletin for Biblical Research* 25 (2015): 55–79.

71. Terence L. Nichols, "Miracles in Science and Theology," *Zygon* 37 (2002): 703.

72. Howard C. Kee, *Medicine, Miracle, and Magic in New Testament Times* (Cambridge University Press, 1986).

73. See especially N. T. Wright, *The Resurrection of the Son of God* (Fortress, 2003). See also Michael R. Licona, *The Resurrection of Jesus: A New Historiographical Approach* (IVP, 2010); Stecher and Blomberg, with Carrier and Williams, *Resurrection*, 80–107, 125–51, 180–91, and 220–61; and Gary Habermas, *Risen Indeed: A Historical Investigation Into the Resurrection of Jesus* (Lexham, 2021).

LEXHAM PRESS

CLARIFYING ANSWERS ON QUESTIONS FOR RESTLESS MINDS

Series Editor: D. A. Carson

The Questions for Restless Minds series applies God's word to today's issues. Each short book faces tough questions honestly and clearly, so you can think wisely, act with conviction, and become more like Christ.

Learn more at lexhampress.com/questions